INSTANT SERENITY FOR

LIFE AND WORK

An introduction to Sophrology

Florence Parot

Light Bubble Publishing
The Panorama
Park Street
Ashford
Kent
TN24 8DF

www.light-bubble-publishing.co.uk

Published by Light Bubble Publishing 2016

ISBN 978-1-911564-00-3

To my children for their everyday love and support

To my students, past, present and future,

you are my inspiration.

CONTENTS

PREFACE

When Florence Parot asked me to write the preface for her book, I was really touched. As I am when I see her infectious enthusiasm and energy for sharing sophrology.

Florence, who trained at my friend Dr Luc Audouin's school in Paris, opened the first training school for sophrologists in the UK in 2010. It makes sense, therefore, that she should be the first one to offer the British public a book on sophrology.

To describe sophrology in a simple and practical way is no mean feat. Yet, Florence has taken up the challenge. She gets straight to the point, in a very pragmatic way that makes her book both appealing and accessible.

I recognise in her approach to sophrology the personal touch of Dr Luc Audouin, in an everyday context. It is essential indeed to give simple and practical tools that will enable the reader to personally feel the purpose of this original method.

Sophrology was born more than 50 years ago in an old provincial hospital in Madrid, Spain. It was in October 1960, when he was still a young doctor, that Alfonso Caycedo decided to initiate a new science of the consciousness and to give it a new name.

It all started with a question, linked to a feeling of inadequacy when working with patients suffering from severe psychiatric disorders and confronted with their sufferings in post-war Spain, with no efficient therapeutic means. This deep, radical question still has not found a definitive answer for the founder of sophrology. It was: "How could I know human consciousness?" To attempt answering this radical question, sophrology has studied "voluntarily modified states of consciousness" through methods such as clinical hypnosis, relaxation, Yoga, Zen, etc. But its aim was and still is the study and the conquest of the harmony of being, of existential plenitude.

As you will soon discover, as you read along, the method has now very much left its initial therapeutical context and even though the ambitious project of Caycedian sophrology still lives on, many of its uses are more modest, more immediate, they adapt more easily to the ups and downs of our everyday existence and enable us to live a more serene life.

Nevertheless, it would be a pity to content yourself with reading the various suggestions in the book. For us, sophrology is before all a practice, an experience and we invite you to take advantage of this guide to start on your own path of discovery.

If those discoveries, those initiations make you feel like you would like to go further, having sessions with a qualified practitioner will be necessary.

I wish you an enjoyable read and practice of some of the exercises suggested in this beautiful book.

Pascal GAUTIER

Psychologist, sophrologist, author

Director of the Rennes Institute of Sophrology

www.sophrologie-formations.com

INTRODUCTION

HOW I CAME TO DISCOVER SOPHROLOGY

I was studying for my two-year Master's Degree in Conference Interpreting at Paris University and my brain was working non-stop. From age 15, I had focused on becoming a Conference Interpreter and all my energy had been on that one goal. I had lived and studied abroad for years, sometimes studying for two qualifications at the same time, in order to be prepared for the final degree. Day after day, for hours on end my fellow students and I were listening to hours of international speeches and interpreting them in another language; our brains having the difficult task of understanding in one language and expressing the same ideas in another one without any time to think about it. That is not counting the constant updating of international politics, economics, law... we had to do. For the first time in my life, I could feel my brain like a muscle, I could feel it ache and overwork. But did I listen to it? Of course not! What do you think, I was no wimp and I knew I was going to be successful. Of the 40 selected students, several had to drop off the course during the 1st year, one by one. We would see them leave, go into therapy, become unwell... After my brain, my digestive system started to show signs of wear and tear. The intense efforts had affected it and I was experiencing stomach pain and discomfort, feeling even slightly dizzy sometimes, so slightly I sometimes thought I was imagining it... There again, I discarded all of it and I just started working harder. The first year ended and the summer holidays arrived. A bit of rest? No sir! Off we went to other countries to work on our languages. I spent most of my summer at Madrid University studying hard under the blazing sun. Autumn was with us and we were preparing for our 2nd and (last) year entry exam, working harder than ever. After all, I was young and healthy and my life was interesting and exciting. Success was at hand! When you love what you do, you can find the energy for it, can't you?

Except that one morning, a few days before the exam, I burnt out... I got up from bed only to fall in a heap on the floor unable to stand up again. An ambulance was called and I was whisked off to A&E. I spent two weeks in hospital with doctors at a loss about my condition. When I came back home, I was so weak I was finding it hard even to get up. I was then diagnosed with Irritable Bowel Syndrome (IBS) and extreme fatigue. I would wake up at night screaming with pain and anxiety. I took the exam later and failed; my brain and body completely unable to function. For a whole year, my life was at a standstill...

Fortunately, after a couple of months of medication, my French GP recommended sophrology. I had no idea what that was at the time but I was prepared to try anything. I loved it. It basically saved me. I looked around, asked questions (no internet search at that time!) and ended up finding group sessions near me. Once a week, for one hour, I would join in a sophrology group session with about 20 others. The sophrologist running the session was a lovely lady, with a soothing voice and great presence. I felt I was in the right place. For about half an hour, we would do small movements and breathe deeply and then we would lie on mats and listen to her voice guiding us in a relaxation exercise. Then we would discuss what we had felt during the exercises, according to what we wanted to share that day. It felt very peaceful. My brain was learning to rest, I was learning how to control my anxieties; my body was calming down, my whole self felt more at ease, serene and energetic at the same time.

I went along to the sessions for several months. After a while, I was able to use many exercises on my own and just went on integrating them here and there in my life according to my needs. I was able to manage the pain from IBS and eventually I was able to get rid of the symptoms and crises and to do without the medication. I was able to function again properly in life. Step by step, I was becoming me again, regaining my confidence and letting my inner light shine once more. I went back to see a sophrologist several times in the coming years, when times were a bit rough and also for prenatal sophrology, both times I was pregnant. I felt able to face life in better way, stronger, empowered.

In case you were wondering, I never became a Conference Interpreter but I started working in international business with the most amazing people, Managers, Chairmen (and women!) who taught me a lot. I used the techniques I had acquired to manage my stress and know myself and my limits and I was able to stay calm and focused among the ups and downs of corporate life.

The day came when I realised it was my turn to give back what I had been given, I retrained to become a sophrologist and started working from a clinic in Paris. Most of my clients are very busy business people under pressure, experiencing stress or insomnia. Some have experienced burnout, many are on the verge of it and all of them have realised how some very simple exercises have turned their lives around and helped them manage their lives and work at full speed while remaining serene and sane. I moved to the UK in 2009 and I am now dedicating my time spreading sophrology there, seeing clients and training sophrologists. This book is intended to give you some idea of what sophrology is and how it can help you find inner peace in a very simple, modern, quick and easy way.

GUIDELINES TO THIS BOOK

This book is meant both as an introduction to sophrology and as a practical guide for everyday life and the work place. You will therefore find a sample of exercises that you can use when you feel the need. These are simple exercises to help you in your everyday life. Pick and choose, mix and match what feels right for you when you need it and enjoy.

Some sophrology exercises are performed standing up and some sitting down, either sitting back or with an upright back. If you cannot stand or are too ill to even sit up, you can lie down. Always do whatever feels more comfortable for you.

Some exercises in this book are for 'instant serenity', they are short and simple and you can incorporate them in your daily routine. Others are longer and will need you to take a 15-20 minute break. For these exercises, you may find it easier to be guided. You can either record yourself or download our exercises online (www.light-bubble-publishing.co.uk)

Do the exercises at your own pace – always be very gentle with yourself and do what feels possible – we have a variety of different tools so start with what feels right for you, the idea is to try different ways and see what works for you, we are all different! Remember, if you need more help, do consult a sophrologist who will be able to guide you in more depth and who will have a clear idea of what exercises are right for you.

WHAT IS SOPHROLOGY?

"There is a middle ground in all things."

Horace

WHAT DOES IT MEAN?

The word sophrology is based on the Greek words:

SOS: harmony

PHREN: consciousness

LOGOS: study or science

It can therefore be described as the study of consciousness in harmony. It is a healthcare philosophy made of very practical physical and mental exercises aiming at an alert mind in a relaxed body.

Professor Alfonso Caycedo, who created it, declared in 1970 during the first International Sophrology Conference:

"Sophrology:

intends to study scientifically the human consciousness,

is both a philosophy and a way of life,

is both a therapy and a personal development technique."

He later added: "Sophrology is learning to live."

The idea of sophrology is to be able to stay both calm and alert in the middle of our modern fast-paced very full life without having to spend a long time doing postures or meditating while sitting down cross-legged. It is ideal for people who feel they do not have the time to do it. Sophrology is often thought of as being a relaxation technique but in fact, relaxation is only one of the tools we use. Other sophrology tools can help regain energy for instance. So the best word to describe sophrology would probably be « balance ». Sophrology can very aptly be described as a technique restoring balance in our body, mind and spirit.

HOW DID IT ALL START?

Professor Caycedo (of Spanish Basque origin, born in Bogota, Colombia in 1932), neuropsychiatrist, created sophrology in 1960 while practising medicine at Madrid Provincial Hospital in Spain.

He originally set out to find a way of healing depressed and traumatised clients by leading them to health and happiness with the least possible use of drugs and psychiatric treatments. He also wanted to study human consciousness and the means of varying its states and levels. He started looking into clinical hypnosis, phenomenology and Western relaxation techniques: Jacobson's progressive relaxation, Schultz's autogenic training. From Jacobson, he mainly kept the idea of differential relaxation: use only the minimum muscle tension necessary to do something and reduce anxiety by relaxing muscular tension. No suggestion or psychotherapy, just muscular relaxation for mental peace. With Schultz's autogenic training, which is a more 'mental' method, he was inspired by our ability to relax by imagining it, by visualising it. In October 1960, he created the word 'sophrology' and opened the first department of clinical sophrology at Santa Isabel Hospital in Madrid.

In 1963, he married a French yoga enthusiast. Although we know little about his private life, this probably explains why he started looking into Eastern techniques around that time.

Between 1963 and 1964, he worked under the psychiatrist and phenomenologist Ludwig Binswanger (who had studied with Husserl and Heidegger) in Switzerland and was very much influenced by his work.

Then, intrigued by the works of yoga and encouraged by Binswanger, he travelled to India and Japan from 1965 to 1968 where he studied yoga, Tummo (Tibetan Buddhist meditation) and Japanese Zen. He approached each discipline, theory and philosophy with the intention of discovering what, exactly, improved people's health, both physically and mentally, in the fastest possible time and with lasting results. He first travelled to India where he discovered Raja Yoga in the ashram of

Swami Anandanand and Sri Aurobindo's integral yoga. He then travelled to Dharamsala to meet the Dalai Lama and study Tibetan Buddhism. Lastly, he went to Japan to learn Zen in several monasteries. On his return, he created the first three levels of what he called Dynamic Relaxation. From then on, sophrology started to move away from clinical hypnosis and concentrated more on body work and the presence of the body in the mind. His idea was to help the Western mind use Eastern methods in a simple way, leaving aside the philosophy and religion, not mimicking those techniques for which he has always had the utmost respect but enabling people to experience easily new ways of working on their levels of consciousness.

On his return to Spain, Professor Caycedo settled in Barcelona where he started expanding sophrology. He initiated sophrology groups in Paris and spread the word at scientific conferences in Spain, Switzerland and Belgium.

In Switzerland, Dr Raymond Abrezol discovered the unique benefits of sophrology and brought it to the attention of the general public. In 1965, having just finished his sophrology studies, he tried to help a friend with whom he was playing tennis regularly. His performances and concentration developed quite dramatically. Abrezol then helped another friend with his skiing performance. A dramatic improvement there again. In 1967, a national ski coach, having heard about it, asked for his help to train four ski champions for the Grenoble Olympic Games of 1968, in great secrecy. Three of them ended up on the podium with Olympic medals. They were the only Swiss champions to receive medals at the Games that year. The athletes revealed their sophrology training to the press. The press were ecstatic and Abrezol ended up training the whole national team from the next season. Medals started pouring in for Switzerland. Funnily enough, after the world championships in 1970, the Ski Federation asked Abrezol not to stay with the skiers at starting point, arguing he had too much influence on them and was "creating a disadvantage for other nations"! Abrezol went on to train many other athletes in sailing, boxing, cycling, tennis, water-polo, golf, etc. Athletes coached by Dr Raymond Abrezol between 1967 and 2004 won over 200 Olympic medals.

Following this success, sophrology grew rapidly throughout the French-speaking world. Although initially used only in medicine, sophrology then opened to other areas: sports of course but also prevention and promotion of health in the corporate world, in education, in the arts, etc. Dr Abrezol ran trainer training programmes for a large number of influential doctors and sports coaches, many of whom now run Training Centres throughout France. His enthusiasm and his success with athletes opened doors for sophrology to be taught in many areas of life.

During his stay in Colombia in 1985, Caycedo created the fourth Level of Dynamic Relaxation and the « social » branch of sophrology. In 1988 he moved to Andorra and created the notion of « Caycedian Sophrology ». In 1992 he started the subsequent levels and created a Master's Degree. In 2001, the twelve levels of Dynamic Relaxation were finished but the first four remain the most commonly used.

Sophrology is now a very popular method in France, Spain, Italy, Switzerland and Belgium and is becoming better known all around the world. It is used in a large variety of disciplines:

The medical branch:

- Obstetrics (prenatal)

- Psychotherapies, depression, phobias, addictions, anxiety and panic attacks...

- Anaesthetics, preparing for an operation, pain management, oncology, palliative care, terminal illnesses

- Sleep disorders

- Chronic fatigue syndrome, fibromyalgia, ME, IBS...

The socio-prophylactic branch (wellbeing, self-development, stress management):

- Sports: self-confidence, motivation, team building, concentration, performance, energy levels, technical difficulties, nerves and pressure...

- Education: artists (creativity, stage fright management, memory, expression...), general education (concentration, motivation, preparing for exams, technical acts...)

- Social and corporate: stress and burnout management,

repetitive strain injuries, body and mind tensions, managing performance and energy levels, change management, preparing for interviews, exams and public speaking, self-confidence, emotions management, self-development, interpersonal skills, inner resources, weight problems and self-image.

We have seen that sophrology is at the crossroads between Eastern and Western methods but it is not a melting pot of techniques where you would mix and match a little bit of yoga with some meditation, a drop of hypnotherapy and a sprinkle of Zen. Rather, its tools and methods are inspired by these techniques but are reframed in a very modern and original way. They work in the same direction but the idea is to have tools that are easy to use for all, easy to remember and very much adapted to our modern world.

HOW IS THE METHOD ORGANISED?

Caycedo has divided sophology in 12 levels, organised in 3 cycles.

1st cycle – The Reductive Cycle

Dynamic Relaxation Level 1:

Inspired by yoga (Raja Yoga and Yoga Nidra mainly), this level concentrates on the body: how do I feel in my body, who am I inside? We become more aware of the body we are living in. We are focusing on the present. We are introduced to relaxation in movement, body work and breath work, creative visualisations and symbolic stories.

The goals are to get rid of our tensions, find inner harmony, improve our relationship with ourselves and develop our body awareness.

Dynamic Relaxation Level 2:

Inspired by Buddhist contemplation techniques, this level focuses on the mind. We contemplate ourselves as if from the outside (what am I?). We also take a positive view of the future, focus on goals, projects, future events, etc. The notions we work on in this level that are coming directly from Buddhist meditation are: peaceful mind, contemplation of inner or external object, non-attachment.

The goals are to improve our relationship with others, developing our five senses and our intuition, be able to stand back, see things from a distance, let go.

Dynamic Relaxation Level 3:

This level is inspired by Japanese Zen and focuses on the interaction between mind and body. We become more aware of the world around us, meditate, try to get to know the reality of things with a non-judgemental attitude and to experience the world as if seeing it "for the first time". We also work on investigating the positive aspects of our past.

We experiment with sitting meditation and walking meditation and awareness even in every moment of everyday life.

Dynamic Relaxation Level 4:

In this fourth level, we return to the here and now, to awareness of our life, our place in society, to feeling alive in the world, in everyday life. We focus on what our values are in life.

2nd cycle – The Radical Cycle

(Levels 5 to 8)

During this cycle, sound (the voice) is used to activate the body, mind and spirit. We focus on the awareness of the vibrations in different parts of our body.

3rd cycle – The Existential Cycle

(Levels 9 to 12)

We learn to live in full consciousness and to understand and be fully aware of the existential values of life: liberty, individuality. We continue to train to be fully present in each moment in time, but also to be aware of all the dimensions of space and time and to be fully in tune with ourselves, the world around us and the universe.

WHAT ARE THE PRINCIPLES OF SOPHROLOGY?

OBJECTIVE REALITY AND NON-JUDGEMENT

Alfonso Caycedo looked into phenomenology after working in 1963-64 with the Swiss psychiatrist Binswanger (1881-1966) who had studied with Husserl and Heidegger. Phenomenology had a big impact on sophrology. Some of the techniques in sophrology suggest we look at things "as if for the first time", with a neutral approach, listening to sensations with no judgement or expectations. Experiencing is key. Suggestion is left to a minimum to let each person experience the exercise in their own ways.

Key concepts are:

- a non-judgemental attitude: look at things with as "neutral" a look as possible, not using our previous knowledge or experience;

- a beginner's mind: look at the world with a child's mind, take it as it is;

- acceptance: accept reality around us and others as they are, without ready-made ideas. Never assume.

POSITIVE ACTION

In sophrology, we do not focus on the problem itself or on the causes, we do not ignore the problem but, to better solve it, we concentrate not on it but on the positive elements inside us and in our past, present or future that will enable us to move forward, to strengthen and reinforce the self, to reach our full potential. The assumption is that positive thoughts start a positive chain reaction inside us. According to Caycedo, "any positive action on part of our consciousness affects our entire being." We ask ourselves: What makes me feel great? What brings me joy? Where do I take my energy from? And we use that knowledge.

According to Pascal Gautier, Director of the Rennes School of Sophrology: "Through an everyday practice, sophrology aims at harmony in human beings: quite a feat! In practice, it does not mean seeing life through pink-tinted glasses but putting an end to an unrealistic or negative vision of life to see things as they are (as much as possible) and reinforce whatever positive we have in us."[1]

BODY AWARENESS

In sophrology, we are exploring our inner self, body, mind and spirit. Sophrology gives us balance thanks to a gentle and better understanding of our body, a calm and peaceful visit of our own body. We make this territory truly our own. We call it integration of the body awareness. First and foremost, the aim is to know ourselves better, to meet with our deeper self, to be more at ease with ourselves, to accept ourselves the way we are.

We want to feel fully alive here and now, to bring the body into a live reality, to live in good health and achieve harmony between body, mind and spirit. We want to get in touch with our body, improve our body perception, enjoy feeling alive. Caycedo talks about « vivencia », which we could translate as « aliveness »: we feel fully and joyfully alive.

HOW DOES IT WORK?

LEVELS OF CONSCIOUSNESS:

In sophrology, we work in a state that could be called a state of relaxation, in between awake and asleep, that we call sophro-liminal level. In that state, the mind is so calm that the intellect won't have its say. It is easier to work on exercises with symbols and images, it has more impact, there is no « little voice ». It quiets the inner « mind chatter », in order to connect with our deeper, wiser intuitive mind. We are able to use a greater part of our brain.

INCREASED RESILIENCE:

Sophrology increases resilience. Let's imagine that we are like a glass full of water. In psychotherapy for instance, you "stir" to let what is not going well resurface, you search the past. In sophrology, you make the glass stronger so that it cannot break anymore, whatever storm is

---

1 Pascal Gautier: *Découvrir la Sophrologie (InterEditions)*

happening inside. Associating psychotherapy and sophrology can in some instances be an amazing catalyst, helping the person understand and heal, gain clarity and resilience. Some people suffering from phobias for instance come to sophrology after or at the same time as psychotherapy because the therapy has enabled them to understand why they have a phobia but they are still suffering from it. Sophrology helps them change the way their mind and body react to what is for them a highly stressful situation and live a more peaceful existence. Sophrology reinforces the whole person; it makes us stronger, more able to resist life's hardships with a greater serenity. Clients say that when "something goes wrong" in their lives, they are feeling bad for a shorter period of time and with less intensity, they recover more quickly.

TOOLKIT: OUR BASIC TECHNIQUES

"Everything that happens in the mind has a physical representation in our brain. Everything that happens in the brain correlates with what happens in our body."

Deepak Chopra

BODY SCAN: BECOMING MORE AWARE OF OUR BODY

"Take good care of your body if you want your soul to feel like living in it."

Chinese proverb

In most sophrology exercises, we take time to become aware of our body, to focus on it bit by bit, checking in. If we notice some tensions, we try to relax them, the best way we can, never forcing anything, not trying too hard. In sophrology, we usually work from head to toe, concentrating in turn on all our body parts.

This can be done very simply, naming the body parts (either the sophrologist guiding you or you can name them mentally in your head). After a few years, Caycedo also decided to group together the parts of the body in sections or « systems » which can be used to focus more quickly on the body. Each system has an « integration point » which is a reference point symbolising the whole system. With practice, simply concentrating on the integration point will relax the whole system.

Sometimes, relaxing that way can seem like a real challenge and some people will find it more difficult than others. If you tell yourself to « just relax », if you are not trained, it is highly probable that nothing will happen. Indeed, if you are told so by someone else, it is even more difficult! You have to learn how to relax. If this is the case for you and you feel you are a very active person, not at ease with sitting down and trying to relax your muscles, why don't you try our dynamic relaxation first? It is also true that, like all our tools, this will get easier with practice. All our exercises are easy but they will be all the more efficient when you need them if you have practised them at least a little bit beforehand when feeling ok.

SYSTEMS	INTEGRATION/ FOCUS POINT	ORGANS
Head + face	Forehead	Brain & Senses
Neck + shoulders + external arms & hands	Base of the neck	Thyroid & Vocal chords
Chest + back + inner arms & hands	Sternum	Thymus, Lungs, Heart
Abdomen + lower back	4 cms above bellybutton	Digestive system, Kidneys, Liver, Spleen
Lower abdomen + legs	4 cms under bellybutton	Reproductive organs
Whole body	Bellybutton	All organs

But remember also that we do not focus on our body just to relax it. Being very simply aware of it is very important. Connecting with our body helps us feel fully alive, in the here and now, in 'real life', not always in our head. So just being aware of your body, even if only to acknowledge that it feels tense, is a very important step.

TRY IT FOR YOURSELF

BASIC BODY SCAN

Sit down in a comfortable position and close your eyes. Take a few moments to feel your body as a whole from head to toe, especially the places where you are in contact with the chair, simply the way your body is placed.

Now, you are going to let your body relax, as much as you can, the best way you can, bringing your awareness to each and every part of your body, starting with the head.

Focus on your face and imagine your forehead is very calm. The entire area around your eyes is relaxing. Soften your cheeks, your jaw muscles. Unclench your jaw, let it relax. Your whole head is calming down. And your mind itself is quieting. If ideas come and go, let them simply flow past or imagine you are putting them in a bag outside the door, you don't need them right now and you can deal with them later. If your mind wanders off, bring it back every time. You can also imagine that you are blowing those ideas away, you get rid of them and you concentrate back to relaxation, to how you are feeling inside.

You are going to move down to your throat and neck and let go of any tensions in this part of your body. Your throat is expanding as if to let more air through. All your neck muscles are unknotting, profoundly, as if your neck was somehow becoming longer and softer.

Let the relaxation flow down to your shoulders, let go of them as if they were dropping gently to the floor. Relax your arms, your elbows, forearms, your wrists, and your hands right through the tips of your fingers.

Let the relaxation get to your back from the upper back down to the base of your spine as if every single back muscle was unknotting one after the other. As if the whole back was breathing out loudly, happy to rest at last.

Now bring your awareness to your chest. You are breathing gently and freely and your heart is beating calmly.

Feel relaxation spreading throughout your stomach, abdominal area. Feel the whole area becoming smooth and calm and all organs inside working together in harmony.

Now move down to the lower part of your body to your hips and legs. Your legs are just resting there, nice and quiet. Feel the relaxation deep into the muscles of your thighs, legs, calves, ankles and feet down to your toes, down to the soles of your feet.

You are aware of your whole body from head to toe.

Take a little time to simply listen to your body, to how you are feeling now.

Now, without opening your eyes yet, you become progressively aware of the environment, of where you are, of all the elements surrounding you here, the furniture, the temperature of the room, noises... Gently start moving your toes, legs, fingers, arms, move your shoulders, neck, head... gently stretch, rub your hands and yawn if you want to and when you are ready, open your eyes.

BASIC BODY SCAN WITH SYSTEMS

Sit down in a comfortable position and close your eyes. Take a few moments to feel your body as a whole from head to toe, especially the places where you are in contact with the chair, simply the way your body is placed.

Now, you are going to let your body relax, system by system, as much as you can, the best way you can, bringing your awareness to each system in turn.

Focus on your first system: the head and face and imagine your forehead is very calm. The entire area around your eyes is relaxing. Soften your cheeks, your jaw muscles. Unclench your jaw, let it relax. Your whole head is calming down. And your mind itself is quieting. If ideas come and go, let them simply flow past or imagine you are putting them in a bag outside the door, you don't need them right now and you can deal with them later. If your mind wanders off, bring it back every time. You can also imagine that you are blowing those ideas away, you get rid of them and you concentrate back to relaxation, to how you are feeling inside. Imagine your brain itself is relaxing.

Focus on your second system: your neck and shoulders as well as the external part of your arms and hands. Your throat is expanding as if to let more air through. All your neck muscles are unknotting, profoundly. Your shoulders are dropping gently to the floor.

Be aware of your third system: your chest, your back, as well as the inner part of your arms and hands. Focus more particularly on your sternum. Imagine your lungs are expanding and you are breathing more freely and peace and quiet are spreading from your upper back to the palm of your hands. Your heart is beating calmly.

Focus on your fourth system: your abdomen and your lower back. Feel relaxation spreading throughout your stomach, abdominal area. Feel the whole area becoming smooth and calm and all the digestive organs inside working together in harmony, functioning well.

Now move down to your fifth system: your lower abdomen and your legs. Your legs are just resting there, nice and quiet. Feel the relaxation deep into the muscles of your thighs, legs, calves, ankles and feet down to your toes, down to the soles of your feet.

Then breathe out, breathe in and, as you breathe in, stretch your whole body gently while putting your arms up and then relax and breathe out... your arms come back on your lap. Focus on your whole body from head to toe.

Listen to your breathing and each time you breathe in, imagine you are activating a nice and warm energy inside, in your whole body, in all your organs. Feel the life inside vibrating, your whole body very much alive.

And now you take a little time to simply listen to your body, to how you are feeling now.

Now, without opening your eyes yet, you become progressively aware of the environment, of where you are, of all the elements surrounding you here, the furniture, the temperature of the room, noises... Gently start moving your toes, legs, fingers, arms, move your shoulders, neck, head... gently stretch, rub your hands and yawn if you want to and when you are ready, open your eyes.

GENTLE MOVEMENTS: DYNAMIC RELAXATION

We have in sophrology something called « Dynamic Relaxation » which can be seen as a contradiction but is probably one of the most original parts of sophrology. Dynamic Relaxation is performed for the most part standing up and most of it is made of small movements. The idea is not to use the movement as a gymnastic exercise but as a means to concentrate, to focus, to connect with ourselves. In sophrology, we do not have complicated postures but short series of small exercises which can be practised by everyone. Some of them can even be done sitting down if someone is not physically capable of standing up. The examples we are going to give you here are all taken from the first level of Dynamic Relaxation.

TRY IT FOR YOURSELF

Always make sure you are able to do the exercise, if any tension or pain is present, take it into account, do it more gently, never force the movement. If need be, imagine you are doing it more than you are actually able to. Always be very gentle with yourself, take good care of yourself. The idea is not to hurt yourself but simply to sense how you are feeling inside and to reduce inner tensions.

If at any time, you feel too tired, dizzy, just sit down, breathe, take a little time and try again at another time. It is a good idea to start with just one or two dynamic exercises. When you have more practice, you can increase the number of exercises.

Ready? Let's go!

Stand up in a comfortable position and close your eyes. Breathe calmly and slowly, in a way that feels comfortable and natural. Concentrate on your head, arms, upper body, lower body, ending up with the contact of your feet with the floor and checking that there are no unnecessary tensions anywhere. Then focus on your whole body from head to toe.

NECK EXERCISE:

Start with a little nod of the head and gently and progressively make it bigger and bigger.

Then turn you head left and right (as if saying no), starting small and making it bigger and bigger.

Make a little circle with your nose, small at first, then bigger and bigger, as if your nose was drawing a snail from the centre outwards. Do it one way round and then the other way round.

Take a little time to listen to how you are feeling.

SHOULDER EXERCISE:

Breathing in, bring your shoulders up, fists closed. Holding your breath gently, do an 'up and down' movement with your shoulders, as brisk or gentle as is right for you. Then, when you need to, breathe out loudly and let go of shoulders, arms, hands.

Repeat three times.

Take a little time to listen to how you are feeling.

TARGET:

Put one foot forward (in a comfortable position), breathe in while raising your arms up in front of you and bringing the arm corresponding to your foot at the back towards your shoulder, as if you had a bow and arrow. Hold your breath gently while focusing on your body or on an imaginary target in front of you. When you need to breathe, release your arm (as if releasing an arrow) and breathe out loudly. Then let your arms fall back into place. Repeat twice and do three times as well with the other side.

You can do this exercise focusing on the movement itself or you can give it an intention: putting a situation, emotion, etc. in the movement or the target.

Take a little time to listen to how you are feeling.

FOREARMS:

Breathing in, let your hands go to your shoulders, breathing out, let them go back down. Do this for the time that feels right for you. You can simply focus on the movement and the breathing or you can imagine that each time you breathe out you let go of stress, tensions... and each time you breathe in, you let in peace, energy, calm...

Take a little time to listen to how you are feeling.

ROTATING MOVEMENT:

Rotate your upper body from left to right and right to left and let your arms follow this movement freely while breathing normally. Then let the movement stop as if by itself.

Take a little time to listen to how you are feeling.

PUPPET:

Jump gently up and down while letting your body follow the move- ment in a very soft and relaxed way. Make sure you do not have any problems with your knees. Stop when you feel this is enough for you.

Take a little time to listen to how you are feeling.

When you are ready, remember the room you are in, return to the here and now, rub your hands, breathe out, stretch and open your eyes.

RELAXATION

Sophrology considers the person as a whole - body, mind and spirit. It is a holistic method, a mind and body training. We can access more that way. Because sometimes, 'just' working with the mind or with the body is not enough.

It is impossible to feel tense in your mind in a relaxed body and vice versa. We can use this to our advantage, using the body to help the mind and the mind to help the body. When we feel most stressed, we relax the body to calm the mind; when we feel physical tensions, we use the mind to relax the body.

But why is it so important to relax? Maybe you think that actually, you love being under pressure and thrive on adrenaline. Actually, there is a little part of our brain that would love us to think this because it loves going and going. But the truth is our whole system needs rest from time to time to function properly (see the 'Take a break' section).

Or maybe you think that you know just what you need to relax: a good glass of wine and a good movie and, done, you are relaxed. But 'real' relaxation will benefit you a thousand times more than common recreation. It is not just a temporary pleasure, it goes even deeper than that, the effects will not be gone in the morning. When relaxing, you make a conscious choice to do so, you follow a method, you are focused and you have a purpose. You deliberately work on your level of consciousness for a particular reason. You take time to connect with yourself. You favour your general balance and wellbeing in the long term. Relaxation is self-conscious « chill-out »!

By learning how to relax and becoming aware of how relaxed (or not!) you are, with practice, you also become able to consciously change your level of relaxation, alertness and awareness. You are in charge!

Through the body scan, we are able to calm the body to quieten the mind. Through visualisation (see next section), we use the mind to relax the body. But we can also use other tools to that end.

Sophrology is relaxed alertness. Our aim is to fall wide awake!

TRY IT FOR YOURSELF

A quick and easy « on the spot » check

Close your eyes in the position you are in right now and, without changing anything, check how you feel: relaxed? Not relaxed? Do not judge, simply observe. Do you need to change something to feel better? Go ahead! Now, how does that feel? Good? Enjoy it! And then open your eyes of course!

Relax your mind using your body: an excellent tool for anxiety

Breathe in and gently contract the muscles in your whole body, sensing any tension or discomfort. Breathe out loudly, let go and completely relax the muscles, letting the tensions flow away. Do this three times and listen to how you are feeling inside. You can do this exercise sitting down, lying down or standing up. Always be very gentle with yourself, do not try to hard.

VISUALISATION

Visualisation, guided imagery,... all those terms cover the same reality: imagining things, places, people and situations in our mind. The idea is to picture them as vividly as we can, making use of our five senses, not just the visual part, with colours, sounds, smells, tastes and even the sense of touch. But even if you think you really are no good at visualising, it is worth a try. There is no one way of doing it. Use one sense more than another if that works better for you, use bits of memories if that helps, take what comes with no judgement, no preconceived ideas. And even if you feel you were only able to visualise for a few seconds, that is great, it means you can try it again!

So why is visualisation such a good tool? As Belleruth Naparstek points out: "Our bodies don't discriminate between sensory images in the mind and what we call reality. [...] Images in the mind are real events in the body. If we combine these three operating principles by (1) introducing images to the mind that the body believes are actual events, and (2) doing this in the altered state, and (3) doing it when, how, and where we want to, we have at our command the unique, powerful, and versatile technique of guided imagery."[2]

The most recent scientific research conducted mainly in the USA with brain imaging of Buddhist monks' brains (the so-called « contemplative neuroscience ») has shown that when we imagine we do a movement, the same area of the motor cortex lights up as when we actually do that movement, just slightly less so[3]. Our autonomous nervous system does not differentiate between a real experience and an experience that we imagine quite vividly.

How useful therefore to have this technique to prepare for a special event for instance: an exam, an interview, a sports event, a stage appearance or simply something we are dreading to do. If we are able to imagine it happening in a positive way, part of our brain will think we have already been able to do it properly therefore, we must be able to do it again properly! We are more confident, less nervous, more able to know success!

In sophrology, when we work with imagery, we always take time to calm

---

2 *Belleruth Naparstek: Staying well with guided imagery (Warner Books)*

3 *Richard Davidson: The emotional life of your brain (Plume Books)*

down, relax our body, then, once we have worked with the image, we let it go consciously and we listen to how we are feeling before coming back to the room, rubbing our hands, stretching and opening our eyes.

TRY IT FOR YOURSELF

LANDSCAPE VISUALISATION

Sit down in a comfortable position and close your eyes. Take a few moments to feel your body as a whole from head to toe, especially the places where you are in contact with the chair, simply the way your body is placed.

Now, you are going to let your body relax, as much as you can, the best way you can, bringing your awareness to each and every part of your body, starting with the head.

Focus on your face and imagine your forehead is very calm. The entire area around your eyes is relaxing. Soften your cheeks, your jaw muscles. Unclench your jaw, let it relax. Your whole head is calming down. And your mind itself is quieting. If ideas come and go, let them simply flow past or imagine you are putting them in a bag outside the door, you don't need them right now and you can deal with them later. If your mind wanders off, bring it back every time. You can also imagine that you are blowing the ideas away, you get rid of them and you concentrate back to relaxation, to how you are feeling inside.

You are going to move down to your throat and neck and let go of any tensions in this part of your body. Your throat is expanding as if to let more air through. All your neck muscles are unknotting, profoundly, as if your neck was somehow becoming longer and softer.

Let the relaxation flow down to your shoulders, let go of them as if they were dropping gently to the floor. Relax your arms, your elbows, forearms, your wrists, and your hands right through the tips of your fingers.

Let the relaxation get to your back from the upper back down to the base of your spine as if every single back muscle was unknotting one after the other. As if the whole back was breathing out loudly, happy to rest at last.

Now bring your awareness to your chest. You are breathing gently and freely and your heart is beating calmly.

Feel relaxation spreading throughout your stomach, abdominal area. Feel the whole area becoming smooth and calm and all organs inside working together in harmony.

Now move down to the lower part of your body to your hips and legs. Your legs are just resting there, nice and quiet. Feel the relax-ation deep into the muscles of your thighs, legs, calves, ankles and feet down to your toes, down to the soles of your feet.

You are aware of your whole body, from head to toe.

And now imagine a beautiful landscape. Maybe a place you know or an imaginary place, it doesn't matter. Try and let an image come, invite an image, encourage it to emerge by itself. Welcome the first image that comes; do not discard it, as long as you feel good in it. If several images appear, wait for a little while, usually, one stays more than the others. If nothing happens, simply choose a landscape.

And that landscape, you can picture it any way you like but try and see it as clearly as you can, try to identify all the elements around you: the colours, with their different shades, brightness or softness, the shapes. Maybe there are smells or perfumes or scents in this landscape. Try and smell them fully. You may also hear sounds, noises. And if you can feel yourself in this landscape, maybe you can touch something, feel the ground under your feet or the wind blowing gently on your face or sun rays on your skin...

Enjoy this moment which is all yours, like a pause, a time to relax and be comfortable. Take time to taste all its delights and how it makes you feel.

And now, you simply let it go, all the images go the way they came. They fade away but you know you can find them again whenever you need. You let them go but you keep all the positive feelings you have experienced through them.

Take a little time to simply listen to your body, to how you are feeling now.

Now, without opening your eyes yet, you become progressively aware of the environment, of where you are, of all the elements surrounding you here, the furniture, the temperature of the room, noises... Gently start moving your toes, legs, fingers, arms; move your shoulders, neck, head... gently stretch, rub your hands and yawn if you want to and when you are ready, open your eyes.

IMAGINING A FUTURE SITUATION

Sit down in a comfortable position and close your eyes. Take a few moments to feel your body as a whole from head to toe, especially the places where you are in contact with the chair, simply the way your body is placed.

Now, you are going to let your body relax, as much as you can, the best way you can, bringing your awareness to each and every part of your body, starting with the head.

Focus on your face and imagine that your forehead is very calm. The entire area around your eyes is relaxing. Soften your cheeks, your jaw muscles. Unclench your jaw, let it relax. Your whole head is calming down. And your mind itself is quieting. If ideas come and go, let them simply flow past or imagine you are putting them in a bag outside the door, you don't need them right now and you can deal with them later. If your mind wanders off, bring it back every time. You can also imagine that you are blowing those ideas away, you get rid of them and you concentrate back to relaxation, to how you are feeling inside.

You are going to move down to your throat and neck and let go of any tensions in this part of your body. Your throat is expanding as if to let more air through. All your neck muscles are unknotting, profoundly, as if your neck was somehow becoming longer and softer.

Let the relaxation flow down to your shoulders, let go of them as if they were dropping gently to the floor. Relax your arms, your elbows, forearms, your wrists, and your hands right through the tips of your fingers.

Let the relaxation get to your back from the upper back down to the base of your spine as if every single back muscle was unknotting one after the other. As if the whole back was breathing out loudly, happy to rest at last.

Now bring your awareness to your chest. You are breathing gently and freely and your heart is beating calmly.

Feel relaxation spreading throughout your stomach, abdominal area. Feel the whole area becoming smooth and calm and all organs inside working together in harmony.

Now move down to the lower part of your body to your hips and legs. Your legs are just resting there, nice and quiet. Feel the relaxation deep into the muscles of your thighs, legs, calves, ankles and feet down to your toes, down to the soles of your feet.

You are aware of your whole body, from head to toe.

Now imagine yourself in a coming future, whether very near in time or more distant, it doesn't matter. But it is a moment you know will come and are expecting with pleasure, you know it is going to be a happy moment. It can be something very simple.

Once you have this moment in mind, imagine it as clearly as possible, and imagine yourself there and everything happening just right. Imagine where you are and what you do, the surroundings, colours, sounds, lights, smells... there may be other people there, you may imagine what people are saying, or any details that make it more real to you. Make it as real as possible, as if it were already happening. Enjoy this moment. Enjoy every bit of it; let it fill you with its joy.

Once you have enjoyed it thoroughly, let the images go, just the way they came. Keep with you the positive feelings that you have experienced.

Take a little time to simply listen to your body, to how you are feeling here and now.

Now, without opening your eyes yet, you become progressively aware of the environment, of where you are, of all the elements surrounding you here, the furniture, the temperature of the room, noises... Gently start moving your toes, legs, fingers, arms, move your shoulders, neck, head... gently stretch, rub your hands and yawn if you want to and when you are ready, open your eyes.

BREATHING

"When we concentrate on our breathing, we bring body and mind back together and become whole again."

Thich Nhat Hanh

Breathing is one of our most powerful tools. Essential to our life, a link between our inner life and the outside world, our breathing is present from birth to death. It is also the only automatic function in our body on which we can act. Studies show that breathing regularly can act like a 'reset' for all the other automatic functions in our body[4]. We can use it anywhere, it is always with us. Working on observing it, focusing on it, becoming aware of it gives us valuable resources both for body and mind.

To work with your breath in sophrology, you do not need to be a trained Yogi. The idea is to use what you are able to do, in the simplest and most comfortable way. So play around with the exercises, take it easy, see how you feel and, as usual, use what works best for you.

TRY IT FOR YOURSELF

With your eyes open or close, become aware of your breathing. Without changing anything, without any judgement or preconceived ideas, simply notice how you breathe. Observe your breath as it flows in and out, follow it. Notice the pattern of your breathing, its speed, its length, if there is a movement in your chest and abdomen each time you breathe in and out. You are simply breathing.

If it helps, you can try putting your hands first on your abdomen, then

---

4 Jerath, R., Edry J.W, Barnes, V.A., and Jerath, V.: *Physiology of long pranayamic breathing*

on your lower chest, then on your upper chest. Simply notice what is happening, try to sense how your breathing is happening, like a discovery, a game.

You could also try following your breathing while standing up, sitting down, lying down, walking... Just to take stock of the possible differences, to see how it feels.

Never force your breathing, let it happen, it does not 'have' to be like this or like that, work with what is comfortable for you. If you are finding it a bit complicated or if you feel you could do with breathing deeper, breathe out deeply and loudly first, through the mouth, then let your breathing go on the way it wants. By emptying the lungs a bit more at first, our body wants to take more air in automatically.

In sophrology, we always breathe in through the nose. We breathe out through the nose or sometimes through the mouth depending on the exercise. But to start with, keep it as simple and natural as possible for you.

CHANGE YOUR LIFE WITH SOPHROLOGY

"Do not walk if you can dance."

Anne Van Stappen

LISTEN TO YOURSELF

"If we are not aware that we are happy, then we are not really happy."

Thich Nhat Hanh

As you will have realised by now, in all sophrology exercises, we take time to listen to how we are feeling, to our sensations. This time, at the end and sometimes during the exercise, gives us time to fully integrate the experience of the exercise. What can happen sometimes is that you may experience a pain or discomfort in one part of your body that you had not noticed before. If you have done the exercise in a gentle way, this is usually not caused by the practice itself, it is rather linked to your listening in, suddenly starting to notice things you were not aware of before. Do not worry and take time to breathe and relax even more to help. In order to help ourselves, we must first be aware of how we are.

Do you know for instance how much sleep you need and at what time? Do you know when you work at your best? Do you know your limits? We need to listen intently inside, to silence the 'background noise' in and around us and concentrate on what we are really feeling. Stop rushing around and listen in.

Knowing your boundaries, your limits is essential. Our body speaks if we know how to listen. We can then stop before it is too late, learn to say no to ourselves or to others, to accept only what is right for us. We are usually told, especially in the corporate world, that we have to adapt to new situations, that it is progress, normal, that if we cannot work harder, longer and better, we are not 'normal'. We are told we need to adapt. But what happens when we reach the limit of our adaptability? Pushing our limits can lead to illness and diseases, fatigue and depression. So by learning to stop before we reach our limit, we are taking care of ourselves, we are learning to live peacefully with ourselves, more aware of ourselves, of our own feelings and sensations. We are also able to preserve our energy.

Making a habit of knowing how we are feeling does not only prevent us from going over our limits, it also enables us to live all our sensations to the full. Joy, love and happiness will taste even better!

TRY IT FOR YOURSELF

Take time to listen to how you are feeling while breathing, driving, arriving home, cooking dinner, eating... Any time during the day when you think about it. You can even create little reminders to keep going during the day.

TAKE A BREAK

"Don't just do something, sit there!"

Thich Nhat Hanh

We all tend to have too many activities to do, one after the other, we are on a roll, trying to get to the bottom of a never-ending to-do list; without taking time to breathe in between. We live in a world where we are over-stimulated all the time, over-adapting: too much noise, light, things to do, to see, too much requiring our attention, too much time spent in front of screens. We are overwhelmed by information. We have to excel in everything we do. Too much pressure, too much of everything. At the end of the day/week/month/year, we are exhausted. We have forgotten to take a break. Would that be a waste of time? Quite the reverse. Our body and mind are not meant to be working non-stop. Only a few seconds of break can make a big difference on your energy levels come the end of the day. You just have to do it! We all need time to switch off and unwind, to shut off the automatic pilot.

Before thinking: "right, what a waste of time!" or "I do not have the time for this!", give it a go, even a 30 second break can recharge you for the rest of the day.

According to a study carried out by the University of California, Santa Barbara, creativity and problem solving are enhanced when day dreaming.[5] Meditation, qi-gong, yoga, sophrology, silent times enhance the immune system, develop our brain in a very positive way: it works faster and better, we can concentrate better, our body works more efficiently. Recent research shows that it develops the left prefrontal lobe of the brain related to wellbeing. What are you waiting for?

Life is a marathon, not a sprint; don't exhaust yourself. As my dad always says: "Be like a cycling champion, keep the energy for the last mile."

TRY IT FOR YOURSELF

Daily Micro-breaks: Several times a day, take a 30 seconds or one minute break. Close your eyes, breathe out deeply, let your shoulders down, forget everything and listen only to your breathing. If you want to make it 2 or 5 minutes, excellent but keep in mind that it is more efficient to have several very short breaks rather than one longer one.

According to Lynne Franks, 'mini breaks' decrease the heart rate and blood pressure and improve oxygen circulation.[6]

Weekly rest: In his marvellous book *The Miracle of Mindfulness*

Thich Nhat Hanh recommends a day of mindfulness and slow living every week. Most cultures and traditions allow for a day off in the week, when we take care of our spiritual life and rest. In our 24/7 world, this is becoming increasingly difficult. We spend our

---

5 *Psychological Science, in Science & Vie, July 2012*

6 *Lynne Franks: Grow: The Modern Woman's Handbook: How to Connect with Self, Lovers, and Others (Hay House UK)*

weekend rushing around doing everything we have not done during the week: shopping, housework, children's activities, 'compulsory' family lunches. As we rush through our week at 2,000 miles per hour, we pour on the weekend what we have not been able to do before and we go for it at the same speed, unable to stop. Here is an idea: keep one day of the weekend (or week if you work at weekends!) to... do nothing! Not always possible, of course. But if you try and put it as a rule that you can sometime overrule, you will have already accomplished a lot. And if you 'have' to do something that day, do it as simply and slowly as possible. Do not plan anything or just ONE thing you love and if on that day you don't feel like doing even that, well, don't! Treat yourself to freedom! No work, no meetings, no friends over, maybe a slow motion bath, a cup of tea, a good book, some soft music, a slow walk, a light simple meal, anything you enjoy doing. Try having a day off everything: alone, at home, with no TV, no phone, no computer... Make sure you are not going to be disturbed and relax. Breathe!

A study by researchers at the University of Rochester, USA, says people feel happier and healthier with fewer aches, pains and symptoms of stress when they spend the weekends doing exactly what they fancy.

Cut on the electronic devices: why not use that weekly break to switch everything off? Computer, mobile phone, everything. You could even put the landline on voicemail. If a whole day seems too much, start with a few hours. You could also do the same thing in the evening, after a pre-defined time. Too much time spent on electronic devices overstimulates the brain. If you want to keep your mind fresh, clear and energetic, let it recharge regularly.

MINDFULNESS

"Simplify, simplify."

Henry David Thoreau

In our very busy lives, we tend to do many things at the same time, always in action, always doing. As children and students, we learn how to do things and are expected as adults to go on doing them. But when are we learning how to simply be? We are human beings, not human « doings ». Learning to be aware of how we are is essential.

In Sophrology, we learn to be mindful of how we are standing, sitting, breathing, eating, feeling. We learn to focus and concentrate. To really live life to the full and enjoy, live every minute of it in a relaxed and peaceful way.

To be mindful is to live in the present, in the now, stop overthinking and mind chatter; do one thing at a time: have you ever tried mindfully washing the dishes or something similar? Slow down. Live a mindful life. Do one thing at a time. Try it and see what happens. Often, when we get better at being in the here and now, time suddenly feels like it is expanding. Multitasking can very quickly become overwhelming. It is also a waste of energy. When we multitask, our brain actually switches from one task to another, never really doing several at the same time, so we spend more time and more energy, our ability to focus on what we are doing is greatly diminished. We think we are being clever but in fact we are tiring ourselves for no reason. Think about it, the word 'present' means 'here' but it also means 'gift'. It is a gift here and now. "Time is not money, it is life."[7]

"It's like going for a walk in a beautiful country road on a summer's day wearing a warrior's helmet. When we stop appreciating the beauty and the possibilities in our lives, we stop believing they are there. It is about the journey as much as the destination, so leave your helmet at home." (Ana Paula Nacif – business coach)

---

7 Erik Pigani: *L'art Zen du temps (Marabout Edition)*

TRY IT FOR YOURSELF

Wash the dishes concentrating solely on it, just that. Make a game of it!

Use your 5 senses: find times during the day when you are fully focused on one of your senses: savour a meal, smell a flower, enjoy the view from your window, listen to music your love, feel your feet on the grass or give someone a hug. Each time, even if only for a few seconds, do it without doing something else at the same time!

MORE TOOLS FOR LIFE AND WORK

"The ideal man is he who, in the midst of the greatest silence and solitude, finds the intensest activity, and in the midst of the intensest activity finds the silence and solitude of the desert."

Swami Vivekananda

In this chapter, you will find a few ideas to help with everyday problems that you can use easily. They are not meant to replace a proper set of sessions with a sophrologist but it is my hope that you will find there some useful tools for everyday life.

IDEAS TO BETTER MANAGE YOUR STRESS

The 'micro break': Several times a day, for a few seconds, close your eyes, unclench your jaw, relax your shoulders (let them drop to the floor) and breathe out.

Waiting = Relaxing[8]: Use any waiting time as compulsory relaxation time: queuing up, stuck in traffic, waiting for someone... instead of wasting your energy getting all worked up, make sure you are breathing calmly and in a relaxed way!

Dynamic relaxation exercises: shoulder exercise, target

The bubbles exercise: Sit down in a comfortable position and close your eyes. Take a few moments to feel your body as a whole from head to toe, especially the places where you are in contact with the chair, simply the way your body is placed.

Now, you are going to let your body relax, as much as you can, the best way you can, bringing your awareness to each and every part of your body, starting with the head.

Focus on your face and imagine your forehead is very calm. The entire area around your eyes is relaxing. Soften your cheeks, your jaw

---

8 *We owe this particularly effective phrase to Dr Luc Audouin, founder of the CEAS School of Sophrology in Paris.*

muscles. Unclench your jaw, let it relax. Your whole head is calming down. And your mind itself is quieting. If ideas come and go, let them simply flow past or imagine you are putting them in a bag outside the door, you don't need them right now and you can deal with them later. If your mind wanders off, bring it back every time. You can also imagine that you are blowing those ideas away, you get rid of them and you concentrate again on relaxing, on the way you are feeling inside.

You are going to move down to your throat and neck and let go of any tensions in this part of your body. Your throat is expanding as if to let more air through. All your neck muscles are unknotting, profoundly, as if your neck was somehow becoming longer and softer.

Let the relaxation flow down to your shoulders, let go of them as if they were dropping gently to the floor. Relax your arms, your elbows, forearms, your wrists, and your hands right through the tips of your fingers.

Let the relaxation flow to your back from the upper back down to the base of your spine as if every single back muscle was unknotting one after the other. As if the whole back was breathing out loudly, happy to rest at last.

Now bring your awareness to your chest. You are breathing gently and freely and your heart is beating calmly.

Feel relaxation spreading throughout your stomach, abdominal area. Feel the whole area becoming smooth and calm and all organs inside working together in harmony.

Now move down to the lower part of your body to your hips and legs. Your legs are just resting there, nice and quiet. Feel the relaxation deep into the muscles of your thighs, legs, calves, ankles and feet down to your toes, down to the soles of your feet.

Focus on your whole body, from head to toe.

Each time you breathe out, imagine that a flow of dark bubbles is leaving your body, taking away with them your worries, stress, anxiety... anything you do not need anymore. Conversely, each time you breathe in, imagine that a flow of golden bubbles is coming to you, bringing you peace, calm or energy or anything else you may be needing at that moment.

Take a little time to simply listen to your body, to how you are feeling now.

Now, without opening your eyes yet, you become progressively aware of the environment, of where you are, of all the elements surrounding you here, the furniture, the temperature of the room, noises... Gently start moving your toes, legs, fingers, arms, move your shoulders, neck, head... gently stretch, rub your hands and yawn if you want to and when you are ready, open your eyes.

IDEAS TO GET A BETTER NIGHT'S SLEEP

To prepare your night during the day:

Several times a day, for a few seconds, close your eyes, unclench your jaw, imagine your lower jaw is somewhat heavier, relax your shoulders (let them drop to the floor), focus on the contact of the soles of your feet with the floor and breathe out.

Dynamic relaxation exercises: target, puppet

If you wake up during the night:

Count up to three in your mind as you breathe in, count up to four as you breathe out and count up to three while you gently hold your breath, your lungs empty and then start all over again. Do this at your own pace and change the counts if this is better for you but keep the exercise as regular as you can until you feel that you are calming down.

Breathe in, very gently contract all your muscles from head to toe and breathe out and let them relax completely. Do this 3 times, breathing out fully each time and relaxing deeply at the same time.

The Bag Exercise:

Sit down in a comfortable position and close your eyes. Take a few moments to feel your body as a whole from head to toe, especially the places where you are in contact with the chair, simply the way your body is placed.

Now, you are going to let your body relax, as much as you can, the best way you can, bringing your awareness to each and every part of your body, starting with the head.

Focus on your face and imagine your forehead is very calm. The entire area around your eyes is relaxing. Soften your cheeks, your jaw muscles. Unclench your jaw, let it relax. Your whole head is calming down. And your mind itself is quieting. If ideas come and go, let them simply flow past or imagine you are putting them in a bag outside the door, you don't need them right now and you can deal with them later. If your mind wanders off, bring it back every time. You can also imagine that you are blowing those ideas away, you get rid of them and you concentrate back to relaxation, to how you are feeling inside.

You are going to move down to your throat and neck and let go of any tensions in this part of your body. Your throat is expanding as if to let more air through. All your neck muscles are unknotting, profoundly, as if your neck was somehow becoming longer and softer.

Let the relaxation flow down to your shoulders, let go of them as if they were dropping gently to the floor. Relax your arms, your elbows, forearms, your wrists and your hands right through the tips of your fingers.

Let the relaxation get to your back from the upper back down to the base of your spine as if every single back muscle was unknotting one after the other. As if the whole back was breathing out loudly, happy to rest at last.

Now bring your awareness to your chest. You are breathing gently and freely and your heart is beating calmly.

Feel relaxation spreading throughout your stomach, abdominal area. Feel the whole area becoming smooth and calm and all organs inside working together in harmony.

Now move down to the lower part of your body to your hips and legs. Your legs are just resting there, nice and quiet. Feel the relaxation deep into the muscles of your thighs, legs, calves, ankles and feet down to your toes, down to the soles of your feet.

You are aware of your whole body from head to toe.

Imagine that you are walking on a mountain path and arriving at the foot of a mountain. On this path ahead of you, you can see a big empty bag and you decide to place in it everything you want to get rid of in your everyday life at the moment, tensions, emotions, blocks, pains... everything you do not need anymore now. You can see all these elements as images, objects, symbols, words, anyway that is right for you. But be aware of each and every one of them, know precisely what you are putting in the bag and breathe deeply and calmly as you do this.

Put everything you want in the bag, make it as full as you want and then take it with you and start climbing up the path that goes to the top of the mountain, looking towards your goal, the light at the top. When you reach the top, you discover this mountain is in fact a volcano and you decide to empty the whole content of your bag in the volcano.

You watch as the lava and flames disintegrate completely everything you have thrown into the volcano, totally, completely.

You go down the path again with your empty bag. On the way down, you take the time to admire the landscape around you, the nature, the flowers, maybe a little mountain spring, birds singing, the sun shining... And when you arrive at the foot of the mountain, you just let all the images go.

Take a little time to simply listen to your body, to how you are feeling now.

Now, without opening your eyes yet, you become progressively aware of the environment, of where you are, of all the elements surrounding you here, the furniture, the temperature of the room, noises... Gently start moving your toes, legs, fingers, arms, move your shoulders, neck, head... gently stretch, rub your hands and yawn if you want to and when you are ready, open your eyes.

IDEAS TO BOOST YOUR SELF-CONFIDENCE

Stand up in a relaxed and comfortable position, eyes closed.

Sense your feet firmly on the floor, the parts of your feet touching the floor and those that don't. Be aware of your upright position. Unclench your jaw, let your shoulders drop towards the floor.

Go back to feeling your feet firmly on the floor, a sense of strength there and imagine that there is a light or coloured energy coming from the ground. Imagine this energy of the earth is flowing up through your feet, legs and all parts of your body and up to your head.

Focus on your breathing and find a comfortable count that will allow you to breathe with four equal times of breathing. For example: breathing in counting up to 3, waiting with your lungs full counting up to 3, breathing out counting up to 3 and waiting with your lungs empty counting up to 3. Do it in a way that is comfortable for you, not too quickly but not too slowly either and for a short time only.

Now imagine you are standing in the sun and breathing in the sun light and energy.

Then let the image of the sun go, breathe out loudly, rub your hands together and open your eyes. How are you feeling?

IDEAS TO BOOST YOUR ENERGY

Breathing in the sun: Sit down in a comfortable position and close your eyes. Take a few moments to feel your body as a whole from head to toe, especially the places where you are in contact with the chair, simply the way your body is placed.

Now, you are going to let your body relax, as much as you can, bringing your awareness to each and every part of your body, starting with the head.

Focus on your face and imagine your forehead is very calm. The entire area around your eyes is relaxing. Soften your cheeks, your jaw muscles. Unclench your jaw, let it relax. Your whole head is calming down. And your mind itself is quieting. If ideas come and go, let them simply flow past or imagine you are putting them in a bag outside the door, you don't need them right now and you can deal with them later. If your mind wanders off, bring it back every time. You can also imagine that you are blowing those ideas away, you get rid of them and you concentrate back to relaxation, to how you are feeling inside.

You are going to move down to your throat and neck and let go of any tensions in this part of your body. Your throat is expanding as if to let more air through. All your neck muscles are unknotting, profoundly, as if your neck was somehow becoming longer and softer.

Let the relaxation flow down to your shoulders, let go of them as if they were dropping gently to the floor. Relax your arms, your elbows, forearms, your wrists, and your hands right through the tips of your fingers.

Let the relaxation get to your back from the upper back down to the base of your spine as if every single back muscle was unknotting one after the other. As if the whole back was breathing out loudly, happy to rest at last.

Now bring your awareness to your chest. You are breathing gently and freely and your heart is beating calmly.

Feel relaxation spreading throughout your stomach, abdominal area. Feel the whole area becoming smooth and calm and all organs inside working together in harmony.

Now move down to the lower part of your body to your hips and legs. Your legs are just resting there, nice and quiet. Feel the relaxation deep into the muscles of your thighs, legs, calves, ankles and feet down to your toes, down to the soles of your feet.

You are aware of your whole body, from head to toe.

Now imagine that you are finding yourself in a very sunny place. Imagine that each time you breathe in, you are breathing in sun rays, sun light, sun warmth and energy, just the amount that is right for you. Let this energy, this warmth into your body and imagine it spreading everywhere, from your head to your arms, your back and your feet. Feel the energising power of the sun and its warmth. Hold this visualisation for a few minutes, then let it go but keep the sensations you have felt.

Take a little time to simply listen to your body, to how you are feeling now.

Now, without opening your eyes yet, you become progressively aware of the environment, of where you are, of all the elements surrounding you here, the furniture, the temperature of the room, noises... Gently start moving your toes, legs, fingers, arms, move your shoulders, neck, head... gently stretch, rub your hands and yawn if you want to and when you are ready, open your eyes.

IDEAS TO LET GO OF ANGER

Dynamic relaxation exercises: karate

The cushion exercise: Standing up, take a cushion, close your eyes, breathe in and imagine you are putting all your anger in the cushion as well as anything that may be annoying you (stress, tensions, anxiety…. anything!). Then breathe out loudly while throwing the cushion on the floor. Pick the cushion up and do it twice more. Then, the third time the cushion is on the floor, stay with your eyes closed for a little while to listen to how you are feeling. When you are ready, breathe out, rub your hands and open your eyes.

IDEAS TO CONCENTRATE BETTER

The neutral object: Sit down in a comfortable position and close your eyes. Take a few moments to feel your body as a whole from head to toe, especially the places where you are in contact with the chair, simply the way your body is placed.

Now, you are going to let your body relax, as much as you can, bringing your awareness to each and every part of your body, starting with the head.

Focus on your face and imagine your forehead is very calm. The entire area around your eyes is relaxing. Soften your cheeks, your jaw muscles. Unclench your jaw, let it relax. Your whole head is calming down. And your mind itself is quieting. If ideas come and go, let them simply flow past or imagine you are putting them in a bag outside the door, you don't need them right now and you can deal with them later. If your mind wanders off, bring it back every time. You can also imagine that you are blowing those ideas away, you get rid of them and you concentrate back to relaxation, to how you are feeling inside.

You are going to move down to your throat and neck and let go of any tensions in this part of your body. Your throat is expanding as if to let more air through. All your neck muscles are unknotting, profoundly, as if your neck was somehow becoming longer and softer.

Let the relaxation flow down to your shoulders, let go of them as if they were dropping gently to the floor. Relax your arms, your elbows, forearms, your wrists, and your hands right through the tips of your fingers.

Let the relaxation get to your back from the upper back down to the base of your spine as if every single back muscle was unknotting one after the other. As if the whole back was breathing out loudly, happy to rest at last.

Now bring your awareness to your chest. You are breathing gently and freely and your heart is beating calmly.

Feel relaxation spreading throughout your stomach, abdominal area. Feel the whole area becoming smooth and calm and all organs inside working together in harmony.

Now move down to the lower part of your body to your hips and legs. Your legs are just resting there, nice and quiet. Feel the relaxation deep into the muscles of your thighs, legs, calves, ankles and feet down to your toes, down to the soles of your feet.

You are aware of your whole body, from head to toe.

Now let come to your mind an object, something very simple, that is not attached to any emotion or feeling in particular. We call it a 'neutral' object for that reason: for you, it is just that, an object, nothing more.

Concentrate on this object fully as if it were in front of your eyes and you could see it clearly. See its size, colour or colours, shape, form, texture... If possible (depending on your object) imagine it is rotating and you can see it from all different angles. Keep your focus, this object is the only thing you are thinking about.

When you feel you have done this long enough (it does not have to be very long), let the image of the object go and take a little time to simply listen to your body, to how you are feeling now.

Now, without opening your eyes yet, you become progressively aware of the environment, of where you are, of all the elements surrounding you here, the furniture, the temperature of the room, noises... Gently start moving your toes, legs, fingers, arms, move your shoulders, neck, head... gently stretch, rub your hands and yawn if you want to and when you are ready, open your eyes.

Whenever you are in need of concentration and focus, close your eyes for a few seconds or a minute and remember your object, focus only on it. Then, let it go, rub your hands, open your eyes and back to what you were doing. How much has your concentration improved?

A SESSION WITH A SOPHROLOGIST

"Transforming oneself transforms the world."

Lama Surya Das

You can practise sophrology in one-to-one sessions or in a group.

In group sessions, you discover the methods and are able at the end of each session to start using some of the techniques. A mixture of dynamic and static exercises is often used, alternating sitting down and standing up times. The aim is to discover and improve general wellbeing.

In one-to-one sessions, the aim is to deal with a specific problem you may be facing. They can be one hour or one hour and a half, once a week or once a fortnight. The number of sessions will be different according to each person but a large majority of people will do between 5 and 10 sessions.

A typical one-to-one session will include:

- a consultation with the sophrologist to assess your specific needs and provide feedback on what has happened in between sessions;

- mental and physical exercises, following a tailor-made programme, guided by the sophrologist's voice, relaxation, practical exercises....

- feedback time: sharing how you have felt during the session.

Most sophrologists will give you some exercises to do at home, repeating some of the techniques seen during the session or inspired by the exercises practised that day. Work in a session and homework are both equally important. They build up together. By practising on your own, you are building your own 'toolkit' and you are then able to use the techniques whenever you need them.

You will have noticed that in sophrology sessions, we use no music, candles or special environment. The idea is that you need to be able to redo it on your own, in any environment, in your normal everyday life.

Sophrology is a very gentle method; we respect you where you are, taking it step by step, at your own pace.

The sophrologist suggests, guides, helps you reach a better awareness of yourself. We do not force. The idea is to help you gain more autonomy, be able to deal with life in a better way after that.

CONCLUSION

Sophrology is mainly a very practical, simple to use technique, amazingly effective and powerful and that is the most important thing to remember.

Now that you have discovered the benefits of sophrology, also remember that it is important to practise. The technique will work only if you use it. As you have seen, you do not need to put aside a great amount of time. But you still need to do it! Practise, practise, practise, even if only a couple of minutes a day.

My hope is that in the midst of our very busy twenty-first century lives, sophrology and similar techniques will help us bring some contemplation and stillness into everyday life, helping us connect with our true selves and express our full potential in our life.

I wish you all the very best.

ABOUT THE AUTHOR

Florence is an international expert in stress and sleep management, a performance coach and sophrology practitioner. She helps busy and talented people under pressure to be at their best when they need it most. She teaches them practical tools and strategies to know how to 'switch off' and 'on' at will, remain in control, have energy, focus, a clear head and build resilience. With methods similar to those used by Olympians, she helps her clients develop the brain power of a corporate athlete: their mind at its best.

After going into burnout more than 20 years ago, it was a learning curve for her to understand how to be able to still have the buzzy life she wanted and keep the excitement going while also respecting her own limits. She turned what started as understanding how to cope into an art form, a lifestyle and a career. Sophrology is the one thing that has helped her most with that.

In 2010, she opened the first sophrology training centre in the UK, The Sophrology Academy, based in Kent. It was recognised in 2013 as a centre of excellence by the profession.

Florence is a member of the Editorial Committee of the French magazine *Sophrologie, Pratiques et Perspectives* and writes regularly for several UK publications.

Connect with Florence, learn more about how sophrology can help you feel better every day or how you can train to become a sophrologist via *contact@sophroacademy.co.uk*

www.sophroacademy.co.uk
www.florence-parot.co.uk
twitter.com/sophroacademy
Facebook.com/TheSophrologyAcademy